WITHDRAWN

SOUTH AFRICA

Michael Gallagher

A+

Smart Apple Media

Fitchburg Public Library
5530 Lacy Road
Fitchburg, WI 53711

This book has been published in cooperation with Franklin Watts.

Designer Rita Storey
Editor Constance Novis
Art Director Jonathan Hair
Editor-in-Chief John C. Miles
Picture Research Diana Morris

Picture credits

Action Press/Rex Features: 11. Rodger Bosch/Image Works/Topfoto: 25. Adil Bradlow/Trace Images/Image Works/Topfoto: 24. David Brauchli/Sygma/Corbis: 26. Romano Cagnoni/Rex Features: 8. Mary Evans Picture Library: 14. Louise Gubb/Image Works/Topfoto: 20. Louise Gubb/Saba/Corbis: 18. Martin Harvey/Corbis: 17. Mike Hutchings/Reuters/Corbis: 12. Glyn Krik/Action Plus: front cover tl. Gideon Mendel/Corbis: 21, 27. Richard T. Nowitz/Corbis:19. Charles O'Rear/Corbis: 23. PA/Topfoto: 15. Mike Parks/Still Pictures: front cover tr. Reuters/Corbis: 9, 13. Jorgen Schytte/Still Pictures: front cover b. Sipa Press/Rex Features: 1, 4, 10. The Travel Library/Rex Features: 7. Peter Turnley/Corbis: 22. Nik Wheeler/Corbis: 5, 16.

Published in the United States by Smart Apple Media
2140 Howard Drive West, North Mankato, Minnesota 56003

U.S. publication copyright © 2008 Smart Apple Media
International copyright reserved in all countries. No part of this book may be reproduced in any form without written permission from the publisher.
Printed in the United States

Library of Congress Cataloging-in-Publication Data

Gallagher, Michael.
South Africa / by Michael Gallagher.
p. cm. – (Countries in the news)
Includes bibliographical references and index.
ISBN-13: 978-1-59920-020-0
1. South Africa—Juvenile literature. I. Title.

DT1719.G35 2007
968—dc22   2006027526

9 8 7 6 5 4 3 2 1

CONTENTS

SOUTH AFRICA WAS ONCE *torn apart by the system of racial discrimination called apartheid, which kept people of different colors strictly separated. Today, it has turned its back on the past to become one of the most colorful and diverse nations on Earth.*

A RACIAL MELTING POT

After decades of division and injustice, South Africa's black, white, Asian, and mixed race communities now live equally before the law. Since the end of apartheid in 1994, the state has recognized no fewer than 11 official languages—9 of them indigenous—reflecting the wealth of different cultures that make up a population of some 45 million.

It is important to remember that each color group can itself contain several distinct ethnic groups. The black population, for example, includes members of the Zulu, Xhosa, Sotho, and Tswana peoples. Even the white minority comprises both English speakers and the Dutch-descended Afrikaners. This "Rainbow Nation" looks to countries as far afield as Europe, India, Madagascar, Southeast Asia, and, of course, the rest of the African continent for its ancestry.

CULTURAL REVIVAL

The South African lifestyle is as varied as the citizens themselves. It may involve living in a palatial mansion with a swimming pool or in a simple thatched hut. Ancient arts and traditions are once again thriving—right alongside modern society. While tourists soak up the sun on white sandy beaches, in the townships, African music, dance, and literature are making a comeback. Many arts, such as the "Kwaito" musical style, have been influenced by the years of protest against apartheid.

Apartheid—the separation of black and white people—was a stain on South Africa's history from 1948 until 1990.

CHANGE AND CHALLENGE

The reborn South Africa has a new flag, a new national anthem, and a new determination to make freedom work. In contrast to its turbulent past, it is now one of the most stable countries in Africa, holding regular free and fair elections since the end of apartheid in 1994.

Indeed, South Africa's relatively bloodless triumph over its own injustices has made it an inspiration to other divided countries. However, many challenges remain. Poverty, unemployment, disease, illiteracy, and crime are all major obstacles to overcome. Many problems are, directly or indirectly, the result of the apartheid years. Hence, though now politically equal, South Africans continue in many respects to lead very unequal lives.

NELSON MANDELA
NATIONAL HERO

Nelson Mandela was born in 1918 into a noble Xhosa family. He trained as a lawyer and became involved in politics. Having decided that violence was the only solution to apartheid, he led a campaign of sabotage against the state, for which he was sentenced to life imprisonment. Intense worldwide pressure led to his release after 27 years, and he negotiated with white president F.W. de Klerk to dismantle apartheid. Mandela became South Africa's first black president in 1994. Stepping down in 1999, he has acted as an ambassador for South Africa, helping to combat foreign conflicts and HIV/AIDS in particular.

KNOW YOUR FACTS

Fewer than 1 in 10 South Africans are white, and of those who are, almost two-thirds speak Afrikaans as their first language. Four out of five people are black, and just under a tenth is "Colored," or mixed race. Most Colored people are also Afrikaans speakers. The remainder of the population is of Asian descent or belongs to very small minorities such as the Chinese community.

The flag of South Africa.

2 GEOGRAPHY: A LAND OF PLENTY

APPROPRIATELY ENOUGH FOR SUCH A *diverse country, South Africa's vast territory varies wildly from place to place. Some regions even enjoy different weather systems.*

DREAM LOCATION

At more than 386,000 square miles (1 million sq km), South Africa is as big as the states of Texas and California combined, and it completely surrounds one of its neighbors, the independent kingdom of Lesotho. Located at the very tip of the African continent, its 2,670-mile (4,300 km) coastline spans two oceans. To the west is the cold south Atlantic, while east of Cape Agulhas—the most southerly point in Africa—the warm waters of the Indian Ocean lap its shores.

● These maps show South Africa's position in the world.

WIND, WATER, AND WARMTH

The differing sea temperatures mean that the climate varies hugely inland. In the west, the cooler Atlantic makes for drier weather. Mountains rise behind most of the coastline, beyond which lies a great, arid scrubland plateau known as the Karoo. The Karoo is dry and extremely hot in the summer but can be cold and even icy in the winter. The hot, dusty Kalahari Desert runs up to the Namibian border. However, the eastern edge of South Africa is lush and tropical year-round, while the south coast "Garden Route" area enjoys hot, dry summers and wet winters. This region endures strong winds, which have made for dangerous sea journeys around the Cape of Good Hope.

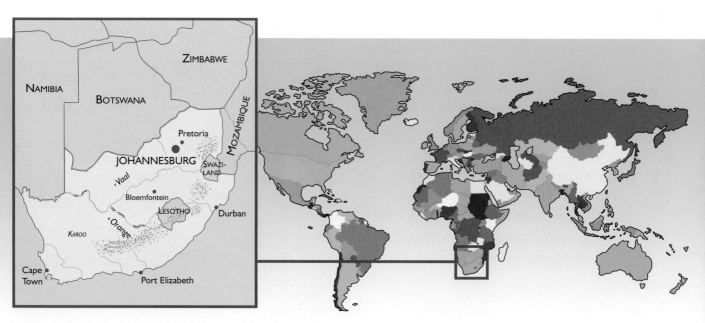

 Part of Cape Town's waterfront, showing Table Mountain in the background.

HISTORIC CITIES

South Africa's big cities reflect the country's natural wealth. The biggest, Johannesburg, was literally built on gold and flourished rapidly after the precious metal was first discovered there in 1886. Today, you can still see the immense waste heaps from the first gold mines around the city, which now has a population of some three million.

Durban, on the southeast coast, is the country's biggest port and home to most of South Africa's Indian population—descendants of indentured laborers brought to work nearby sugar plantations. The oldest city is Cape Town, close to South Africa's only natural harbor. It was here that the first

WHAT DO YOU THINK?

South Africa produces much of the world's gold, plus other precious metals and diamonds. It has huge mineral deposits, prime agricultural land, and is self-sufficient in most staple foods. But many of its people are poorly educated, lack skills, and cannot find jobs. So should South Africa be described as rich or poor? What do you think?

Europeans landed, and hence it is known as the Mother City. Today, Cape Town still boasts the distinctive Cape Dutch style of colonial architecture.

FLORAL DIVERSITY

South Africa is unique in having to itself an entire floral ecosystem—the world's smallest but richest. The Cape Floral Kingdom exists solely within the country's borders and has a greater concentration of plant species than anywhere else on Earth.

SOUTH AFRICA'S MODERN HISTORY *is one of injustice and exploitation. Until recently, violence was the usual outcome.*

ARRIVAL OF THE DUTCH

South Africa's original inhabitants were black Africans, but in 1652, the Dutch settled on the Cape of Good Hope to establish a shipping supply base. They were later joined by German and French refugees, and from these immigrants, the Afrikaner people, also known as Boers, emerged. From the start, the Europeans skirmished with local tribes whose lands they encroached upon. But they also sometimes interbred with them, laying the foundations for South Africa's Colored community. Today, the Colored population is still centered around the Cape.

BRITISH RIVALRY

In the late 18th century, Britain occupied the Cape, and the Boers were driven inland. Eventually, and after bloody conflict with the Zulus, they founded the republics of the Transvaal and the Orange Free State, while Britain created another colony in Natal. Later, the British and the Boers fought a series of wars, which left Britain in control of all four dependencies. In 1910, these were merged into the Union of South Africa. A British act of parliament in 1934 gave whites exclusive control in the Union's parliament.

 Life under apartheid: a white family poses with its black servants.

WHAT DO YOU THINK?

The National Party introduced the system of laws known as apartheid in 1948 and continued it for almost half a century. But racial and ethnic discrimination existed long before then. The British excluded nonwhites from the Union of South Africa government, and in the 19th century, Britain fought ruthlessly against the determination of native inhabitants to govern themselves and their land. Before that, the Boers did the same. So who is to blame for apartheid?

Coffin bearers carry the bodies of blacks murdered by security forces, 1976.

RULE OF THE RACISTS

The British-Afrikaner rivalry continued into the 20th century, but in 1948, the mainly Afrikaner National Party was elected to power. Under its rule, the system of apartheid (literally, "separation") was created. The best land, homes, and facilities were reserved for whites. Even beaches and park benches were segregated. Black people were evicted from their houses and sent to sprawling townships and supposedly independent "homelands." They needed passes to enter white areas and had no say in South Africa's government.

RISING VIOLENCE

The 1950s and '60s saw rising violence against this injustice. In 1961, South Africa left the Commonwealth over widespread revulsion at apartheid. That same year, the antiapartheid African National Congress (ANC) began an armed resistance campaign, and one of its leaders, a young lawyer named Nelson Mandela, was among those later jailed as a result. He was to spend the next 27 years in prison, as South Africa's racial agonies continued.

"We Afrikaners are not a work of man, but a creation of God. It is to us that millions of barbarous blacks look for guidance, justice, and the Christian way of life."
D.F. Malan, leader of the National Party, 1948

KNOW YOUR FACTS

Few politicians today would try to defend apartheid. But for decades, foreign governments did little to stop the horror. Some, such as Britain and the United States, feared that black rule might enable Russian influence in South Africa at a time when Moscow and the West were "Cold War" rivals. Other countries, such as Israel, had important defense industry links to the apartheid regime.

POST-APARTHEID SOUTH AFRICA *could easily have fallen into fresh violence and even civil war. One man's vision helped to ensure that it did not.*

END OF THE NIGHTMARE

In 1990, South Africa and the world watched in admiration as Nelson Mandela walked free after nearly three decades in jail. Crowds cheered, Mandela waved, and a new age of democracy began. South Africa's most famous prisoner was liberated after the white president at the time, F.W. de Klerk, realized that the end of apartheid was inevitable. A global outcry against the system had left the country isolated, its imports and exports blocked. Whites were especially hurt by an international sports boycott. And at home, serious violence had become a daily occurrence. So, de Klerk legalized Mandela's ANC, along with other previously banned groups, and began negotiations toward a free, nonracist state.

DEMOCRATIC MIRACLE

South Africa's transition to democracy was neither easy nor risk free. White supremacist groups tried to derail the process. Some of the security forces were suspected of lending them a hand. And members of the Inkatha Zulu political party initially opposed ANC power, shunning the democratic process for a time. In KwaZulu-Natal there were battles between supporters of the two groups, even as their leaders committed themselves to peace. Some people feared South Africa would split apart or descend into civil war. But eventually, on April 26–28, 1994, black, white, brown, and Colored people lined up patiently to vote in South Africa's first-ever multiracial elections. The result was an ANC-led government, with Mandela as president.

"Never, never, and never again shall it be that this beautiful land will again experience the oppression of one by another."
Nelson Mandela

Nelson Mandela gives the ANC closed-fist salute as he leaves prison in February 1990.

GOODWILL TRIUMPHS

Some whites feared the black government would take revenge upon them for the apartheid years. Yet, despite his own years of suffering, Mandela proved to be a leader of remarkable humanity. He formed a government of national unity, which included white and Zulu leaders. And a special Truth and Reconciliation Commission was set up to find out who was responsible for what during the apartheid years and—in some cases—to pardon them. Today, most South Africans are proud that their country managed to turn its back on injustice so peacefully. And for many, Mandela has become a hero.

KNOW YOUR FACTS

The election of 1994 was a historic occasion, bringing the chance of ethnic reconciliation, but the country still voted along racial lines. About 85 percent of black voters enthusiastically supported the ANC, but almost no whites did the same. Hardly any black votes were cast for F.W. de Klerk's National Party, which attracted most white, Colored, and Indian support.

GROUNDS FOR DEBATE

Thabo Mbeki became president in 1999, winning a second term in April 2004. As deputy president under Nelson Mandela, he also wielded great influence before that. The son of activist parents, he says he was born into the antiapartheid cause, and he spent almost three decades living and campaigning in exile.

However, he lacks Mandela's charisma, and opponents say he has not achieved enough. In particular, Mbeki has been criticized over his refusal to condemn human rights abuses in Zimbabwe and his slow reaction to South Africa's AIDS crisis.

 Thabo Mbeki succeeded Nelson Mandela as president in 1999.

HOW SOUTH AFRICA IS RULED TODAY

TODAY'S SOUTH AFRICANS *live in a stable, democratic country. Yet the first three free elections have given overwhelming power to one party alone.*

ENLIGHTENED NEW STATE

In stark contrast to its past, South Africa is now one of the most liberal countries in the world. The post-apartheid constitution outlaws discrimination not only on the grounds of race, but also of religion, language, gender, and sexuality. The impoverished black "homelands," whose inhabitants were barred from holding South African citizenship, have ceased to exist, and instead, the country is now divided into nine provinces, each of which has its own parliament to deal with local issues.

CHECKS AND BALANCES

The central government, too, has been reformed. A 400-seat National Assembly is elected using proportional representation and then chooses the country's

president, who can rule for a maximum of two five-year terms. The Assembly is monitored by another chamber called the National Council of the Provinces. Unlike most countries, South Africa does not have one capital city but has always split its governing authority between no fewer than three. The parliament sits in Cape Town, while Pretoria is the administrative capital, and the legal center of the country is Bloemfontein.

THE RISE AND RISE OF THE ANC

Within South African politics, the ANC reigns supreme. It won the historic election of 1994, yet even more people voted for it in the next contest in 1997, and still more again in 2001. The beloved hero of the antiapartheid struggle,

A view of the National Assembly chamber.

Jubilant supporters wave the ANC flag.

WHAT DO YOU THINK?

After 1994, the ANC shared some of its power by inviting smaller rival parties into a government of national unity. Later though, the National Party left, saying it had no influence over proceedings. It has since disbanded. Meanwhile, the ANC has struck alliances with other smaller parties to maximize its influence throughout the nine provinces. Critics say this undermines democracy, but ANC supporters point to South Africa's unprecedented political stability. What do you think?

CLOSING THE GAP

In its second decade after apartheid, South Africa remains an unequal society. Even so, enormous progress has been made toward closing the gap between rich and poor. Three-quarters of all households have electricity, and an extra nine million people have access to clean water. More than one and a half million affordable homes have been built. In addition, South Africa has made strides toward paying off foreign debts.

Nelson Mandela, stood down as president in favor of Thabo Mbeki in 1999. Many of the ANC's ambitions for South Africa are, as yet, unfulfilled. But many South Africans still have enormous affection for the party that finally introduced black-majority rule. Others are proud that, in government, the ANC has been willing to act against the wishes of Western countries when necessary.

"It is often said that the first election after freedom is the last one, because most countries degenerate into dictatorships. We are disproving that."
Archbishop Desmond Tutu

MORE THAN THREE CENTURIES OLD,

South Africa's longest-established white community has proved to be as hardy as the land itself. Today, though, a much broader Afrikaner culture is emerging.

INTO THE BUSH

The Afrikaners are a tough and resilient people, unique to South Africa. They are descended from the 17th-century Dutch immigrants who were the first whites to settle there, and even today, their folklore recalls the celebrated "Voortrekker" pioneers who struck out to tame the country's unforgiving interior. The "Great Trek," as it was known, was a response to Britain's occupation of the Cape, and a series of bitter wars ensued when gold and mineral wealth was discovered inland. The Afrikaners' ancestors, the Boers, fought well, despite losing to superior British firepower. They also clashed with native black peoples in order to set up their new colonies. Over time, they developed an intense bond with the land and began to see themselves as African rather than European.

AN INCLUSIVE FUTURE

During the 20th century, Afrikaner nationalism helped to create apartheid, and for decades, the Afrikaners were blamed for the system. With the advent of democracy, they suffered a big loss of

 Boer pioneers trekked to the interior of South Africa in carts drawn by oxen.

status, yet a new Afrikaner identity may now be emerging, based not on color but on the Afrikaans language. Afrikaans is derived from Dutch, with elements of Asian languages brought by slaves, plus local African influences. It is spoken not only by white Afrikaners, but also by Coloreds and some black South Africans. Though once a symbol of white oppression, some people now believe that all who share this diverse language should be considered Afrikaners.

ENDURING CULTURE

Meanwhile, the tough edge to the white Afrikaners' culture remains. Their long association with the great outdoors is still reflected all over South Africa in the country's love of the barbeque, or *braai*, as it is locally known. Unsurprisingly, the preferred ingredient is meat, with favorite dishes like *boerewors*, a spicy sausage.

The Afrikaners have a passion for rugby, and when the rugby World Cup was held in South Africa in 1995, it did much to bring the entire nation together— especially since the home side won. The gentler side of Afrikaner tradition is expressed in a wide body of Afrikaans poetry and literature.

KNOW YOUR FACTS

The Afrikaners were the main beneficiaries of apartheid, but most of them now accept the new multiracial South Africa. Some ultraconservative fringe groups claim whites are oppressed and dream of establishing an independent Afrikaner homeland. However, this is unlikely ever to happen. In the 2004 general election, the right-wing Freedom Front party, which fights for Afrikaner interests, won less than one percent of the vote.

South Africa's rugby team, the Springboks (green shirts) in action against New Zealand.

KNOWN FOR THEIR FEROCITY AND INDEPENDENCE, *the Zulus were united into a powerful empire after 1815 by a leader named Shaka Zulu. Today, they remain one of South Africa's most distinctive ethnic groups.*

STRENGTH AND CONFIDENCE

"Zulu" means heaven, and this proud people might have good reason to believe in divine favor. United by Shaka Zulu's conquest of squabbling farmers and chieftains, they became the largest and most powerful nation in southeastern Africa, even inflicting one celebrated defeat on the mighty British Army. The Zulus' military prowess is still reflected in traditional stick fighting duels called *umshiza*. But there is also a gentler side to their lives.

TIMELESS CUSTOMS

Zulus today are as likely to inhabit a township or a conventional suburb as a village, but some traditional settlements remain. These may be based on the *imizi*, a grouping of huts surrounded by a circular fence. In the past, the huts were round and made of woven reeds, but nowadays more permanent materials are used. Many village dwellers receive money from family members living and working in cities.

Despite modern ways, the Zulus' ancient healing rituals, dress codes, and ancestor worship survive. Social gatherings invariably feature dancing with shields and spears. And beadwork—perhaps the pride of Zulu culture—still thrives. Women create elaborate patterns of colored beads, each of which has a different meaning, and the finished work can convey messages such as an offer of marriage.

 A Zulu woman creates intricate beadwork.

LIVING CULTURE

Under apartheid, the Zulus' territory was made one of the "homelands" to which blacks were restricted, but it has since become part of the modern South African province of KwaZulu-Natal. Even so, the Zulus are still determined to preserve their unique identity. Their leaders often disagree with the national government, and some even threatened not to take part in the first free elections.

Today, the Zulu language is the most widely spoken in South Africa, and the Zulu musical culture has been given worldwide exposure by artists such as Paul Simon and the Zulu entertainment act Ladysmith Black Mambazo.

KNOW YOUR FACTS

King Goodwill Zwelithini is the longest-reigning monarch in modern Zulu history, but his life has not been easy. As a youth he was hidden away to avoid being killed by members of his own family eager to snatch the throne. Then the apartheid government downgraded his coronation ceremony in 1971 to that of a chieftain. The king has had to endure divisions within his own people and tensions between them and the South African national government. But he has retained his subjects' respect by staying above politics and working to preserve Zulu culture. King Goodwill has 6 wives and more than 20 children.

A young Zulu with some of his family's cattle.

8 MINORITIES: COLOREDS & INDIANS

NOT ALL SOUTH AFRICANS ARE BLACK OR WHITE. *The so-called Coloreds number more than three million, and there is a smaller population of Indian descent.*

SECOND CLASS CITIZENS

The term "Colored" is applied to South Africans of mixed race, and they trace their roots to the children of Europeans, Africans, and slaves from both Africa and Asia. A large number are members of the Protestant Dutch Reformed Church, and around 85 percent of them speak Afrikaans as their first language. Under apartheid, Coloreds were given some privileges denied to blacks and often received better jobs and education.

KNOW YOUR FACTS

The ancestors of today's Colored communities include black Africans, but many Coloreds view themselves as quite distinct from the majority black population. Indeed, many feared being sidelined by black rule under the ANC and supported its political rivals after the fall of apartheid. One of their main objectives was to preserve the Afrikaans language.

Black, white, and Colored students enjoy a break together at Cape Town University.

MUSLIMS IN THE CAPE

Most Coloreds live in the Western and Northern Cape regions. Their separate identity helped make the Western Cape the only province the ANC did not control after the 1994 elections. Yet Coloreds belong to several different subgroups. The biggest is known as the Griqua, but perhaps the most distinctive is the so-called Cape Malay community. Based in Cape Town, these people are descended from slaves born in the Dutch East Indies (present-day Indonesia). To this day, they retain their ancestors' customs. Cape Malay dishes, including mild curries seasoned with fruit, are the nearest thing South Africa has to a national cuisine. The Cape Malays also brought Islam with them, and their mosques still compete for space amid the brightly colored houses of Cape Town's Bo Kaap district. Many now see their faith as more relevant than their ethnic background and prefer to be known as Cape Muslims.

A FLAVOR OF INDIA

South Africa is also home to the largest Indian community outside India itself—almost one million strong. Most of these people live in Durban and trace their roots either to indentured laborers brought from the subcontinent by the British in the 19th century or to Indian merchants who followed. To this day, Durban has many Indian restaurants, and its Victoria Street market is alive with handicrafts and spices.

 A colorful Muslim shop in Cape Town.

 Under apartheid, township housing consisted mainly of tumbledown shacks.

APARTHEID RESERVED THE BEST LAND IN *South Africa for whites, and other South Africans were left in poverty. The vast townships remain as testimony to their hardships.*

OPEN PRISONS

Beyond the limits of the white-only suburbs, townships evolved as virtual refugee camps for nonwhites, and their unwilling residents suffered poverty, disease, and overcrowding. They became infamous, both as centers of resistance to apartheid and for riots and violence. Township residents were forced to live in grim working men's hostels or tiny "matchbox" houses, or were confined to shantytowns made of wood and corrugated iron. Today, many still are.

GROUNDS FOR DEBATE

Some people are uneasy that so many years after apartheid ended, townships continue to exist. They believe they are symbols of oppression. But South Africa has limited money to rehouse so many people, and there are even more urgent jobs to be done. Township dwellers themselves sometimes say they are resigned to their fate and that real improvement can only be achieved by their children's generation.

 Minibuses wait to ferry people to work in this township scene.

KNOW YOUR FACTS

The District Six neighborhood of Cape Town is an example of how South Africa is trying to rebuild itself after apartheid. Once a vibrant, though poor, inner city community, 60,000 of its residents were forcibly removed to townships after 1965 so that the area could be redeveloped for whites. District Six was flattened, but the new white suburb never materialized, and for years, the area was derelict and overgrown. Today, houses are once again being built, and some of those evicted are being offered the chance to return.

THRIVING COMMUNITIES

Even so, life in the townships can be colorful. Many have acquired their own distinctive cultures, and some have a thriving nightlife scene, including live music, dance clubs, and drinking establishments known as shebeens. By day, among the dusty tracks and between the jerry-built shacks, township street activity is frenetic. Stalls sell basic household commodities, and enterprising residents offer every service, from fixing TV sets to burying the dead.

Car ownership is very low, so fleets of minibuses ferry workers between their homes and jobs. On days off, workers might play soccer, long established as the main black sport in South Africa.

A BETTER FUTURE?

The sprawling townships are unlikely to disappear anytime soon. The largest, Soweto, outside Johannesburg, has a population of around a million people. But things are slowly improving. More homes than ever now have access to running water, electricity, and sanitation. And a growing number of shacks are being replaced by modest brick houses.

Soweto has become known as the cultural heartbeat of the nation for its flowering of arts and music. Not long ago, the only whites ever to venture here were security forces. Today, even some tourists make the trip, observing the human dignity that has enabled black South Africa to look forward.

APARTHEID MADE WHITES BY FAR THE
richest community in South Africa. How to spread wealth more equally—but without losing white support—is now one of the country's biggest challenges.

UNEQUAL DEVELOPMENT

South Africa accounts for almost a third of the entire African economy. However, most of its businesses are still owned either by the white minority or by international companies. And whites still have many of the best jobs. This is made worse by a lack of skills and even basic education among the black population. This is partly a result of apartheid, since, in protest at inferior facilities, many black people gave up their schooling. Today, some of them have to work in the "informal" economy, doing jobs such as guarding parked cars in return for loose change.

A HELPING HAND

The government is trying hard to change things, though it is a difficult task, especially since foreign investors may be scared away by any sudden upheavals. One solution is to impose targets for the number of black workers companies should employ. Critics say this can lead to unqualified people being appointed to jobs they cannot do. And even if this so-called "Black Empowerment" works, they say, it will only create another small, privileged group of people rather than spreading wealth to many.

GROUNDS FOR DEBATE

Economists once feared that the ANC government might improve the lives of the poor at the expense of big firms operating in South Africa, but the black majority government has always worked hard to keep the trust of investors. Since 1994, it has done little to restrict their freedoms or impose new taxes. Some people say the government has caved in to powerful foreign governments and global corporations. But officials say any other strategy could have meant international companies pulling out of the country, costing many jobs.

Sign of the times: a well-dressed black worker sets off from a nice suburb.

BACK TO THE LAND

Another sticking point is land reform. Many black farmers had their lands confiscated under apartheid, and in 1994, the democratic government vowed to return a third of white farms within five years. But not enough money has been available to help black farmers take up the land; the government has moved very slowly in order to avoid upsetting the economy too much. Today, very little land has been turned over to black ownership, and the original five-year target has been set back to 2015.

Despite its riches, then, South Africa has many economic problems. Today, unemployment is as high as 40 percent, and frustration at the slow pace of change led to a series of strikes and demonstrations against the ANC in 2005.

KNOW YOUR FACTS

Gold mining has traditionally been the preserve of black South Africans and migrant workers—even under apartheid—but it is a backbreaking and dangerous job. Miners work up to 2 miles (3 km) underground in cramped tunnels where temperatures can reach more than 120 °F (50 °C). They have to extract much of the ore from which gold is produced by hand, as there is not enough space for machines. As in the past, most miners still live in hostels near the mines, often far away from their families. It is not unusual for several men to share a single room. Today, with jobs and production in decline, mining unions have become increasingly vocal in demanding improved conditions.

Hot, dirty, and dangerous—a miner digs out ore in a gold mine.

AIDS IS THE SINGLE GREATEST TRAGEDY *facing the African continent today. It affects more people in South Africa than in any other country in the world.*

DEADLY CRISIS

The size of South Africa's AIDS emergency is hard to exaggerate. Some 5.3 million people are thought to be infected with HIV, the virus that causes AIDS. Up to 600 people die every day, and by 2010, 2 million children could be orphans as a result.

Some people fear that South Africa's work force may be decimated because so many people are dying. As with most of the country's problems, the black population is worst affected. In 2005, Nelson Mandela's own son, Makgatho, died of AIDS, as did the son of Zulu political leader Mangosuthu Buthelezi.

KNOW YOUR FACTS

AIDS is caused by HIV, a virus transmitted by contact with some body fluids. It is spread through unprotected sex, not through kissing or touching someone who is infected. Today, powerful drugs can radically slow down HIV's transition to AIDS. But they can be less effective if they are only given once a patient's condition worsens. Those without them at all can quickly become very ill and die.

A PEOPLE BETRAYED

The situation is compounded by attitudes within a poor and ill-educated community. HIV/AIDS is a sexually transmitted disease. Despite this, too many black males refuse to use condoms on the grounds that they are unmanly or because they fear that using them might suggest that they are HIV positive. And too many females are unable or unwilling to insist on safe sex. Meanwhile, fear of AIDS has led to sufferers being victimized, so some people don't want to know if they have HIV, preferring to hope for the best until it is too late. The government, too, has been slow to act. International drug companies gave permission to make affordable

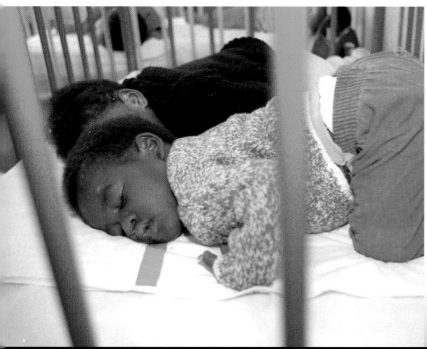

 Children orphaned by HIV/AIDS sleep on a cot at a hospital.

copies of their expensive anti-AIDS drugs as long ago as 2001. Yet officials did not begin giving out the drugs until 2004—and then only after pressure groups warned of legal action.

The drugs—known as antiretrovirals—cannot cure AIDS. However, they extend the lives of patients, and tens of thousands who have died could still be alive today had they received them. Instead, the health minister advised those infected with HIV to take traditional remedies. And President Mbeki even questioned the effects of HIV, saying that AIDS was caused by poverty.

A GLIMMER OF HOPE

Today, AIDS drugs are available through the public health system. But they need to be taken at precise intervals as part of a strict treatment regimen. In isolated rural communities, where very few medical facilities exist, controlling their use is a mammoth task for doctors. Distribution, too, can be difficult. Today, there is at last some hope that AIDS deaths may level off within a few years, but South Africa's best strategy must still lie in prevention rather than cure.

GROUNDS FOR DEBATE

Is poverty the cause of AIDS? President Mbeki famously claimed that AIDS is caused by poverty, and, indeed, knowledge about the disease is lower among the poor, thanks to patchy education and the illiteracy of a large minority. Poor people are also less likely to approach a doctor or to be tested for HIV. But anti-AIDS activists say Mbeki's comment was unhelpful because it distracted people from the need to change behavior and avoid becoming HIV positive.

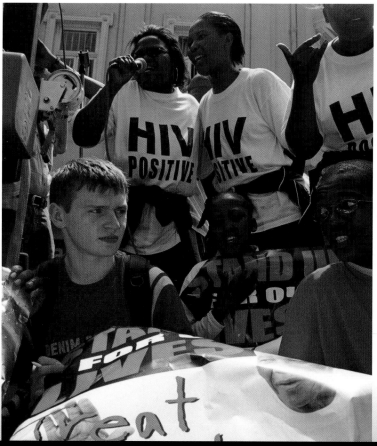

Recent demonstrations have sought to focus government attention on the HIV/AIDS issue in South Africa.

SINCE THE END OF APARTHEID, *violent crime has become a problem for all South Africans. Some people believe it is the country's most serious threat and might even undermine the new democracy.*

CITY OF FEAR

Driving around Johannesburg at night, few people leave their car doors unlocked. Some even refuse to stop at red traffic lights. The reason is a new crime that has arisen in the city since 1994: car hijacking at gunpoint. In the years following the end of apartheid, South Africa has suffered an explosion of all kinds of violent crimes, which has made its cities the murder, rape, and robbery capitals of the world. Though the worst now appears to be over and violence may be stabilizing to some extent, crime is still appallingly high.

Gun crime is a huge problem in South Africa.

WHAT DO YOU THINK?

For many South Africans who can afford it, home is a place behind high walls and security gates. Entire "gated communities" have become common. Some people say living like this is the only way to feel safe. But gated communities do not solve the problem of crime. Indeed, on the other side of the walls, South Africa's streets are often empty and perhaps even more dangerous as a result. Some social commentators add that when the rich look after themselves in such a narrow manner, they are less likely to take an interest in society more generally. So is life behind walls a help or a hindrance in the fight against crime?

 Many of the homes of South Africa's wealthy are protected by electric fences and guard dogs.

FLIGHT OF THE WEALTHY

South Africans of all colors and backgrounds are the victims. According to one poll, more than half said they or someone they knew had suffered at the hands of criminals.

From poor townships to rural farming communities to wealthy suburbs, people speak of crime as a new kind of oppression. It is not uncommon to see homes protected by electrified razor wire, and almost everywhere, signs warn prospective burglars of armed security guards or attack dogs. Those who can afford it have often moved out of the cities or even overseas. A number of businesses have relocated out of central Johannesburg, leaving the city's streets to colorful hawkers and beggars.

TIDE OF ANGER

No one knows for sure why crime is so high. At one point, Thabo Mbeki suspected political extremists were behind much of it, trying to undermine black-majority rule. But it is likely that more complicated factors are to blame.

Many nonwhites felt personally humiliated by their treatment under apartheid; some are still resentful and angry. Deep poverty remains, but the poor are tantalized by the trappings of wealth to be seen everywhere. And, thanks partly to nearby military conflicts, guns are readily available. A high number of South Africans now say they would like violent criminals to be executed. The irony is that in the new South Africa, the death penalty has been abolished.

1652 Dutch colony founded on Cape.

1795 British occupy the Cape.

1816 Shaka becomes leader of the Zulus.

1820s–30s Shaka overcomes his rivals in the Zulu wars.

1836–38 Boers' "Great Trek" in protest of British rule.

1867 Diamonds discovered.

1879 Zulus defeat the British at Isandhlwana.

1899–1902 Anglo-Boer War.

1910 Union of South Africa formed.

1934 Status of the Union Act gives exclusive control to whites.

1948 National Party gains power and establishes apartheid.

1950 Protests against apartheid by nonwhites.

1960 Sharpville Massacre: police open fire on township demonstrators, killing 69 and focusing world attention on apartheid.

1961 South Africa leaves the Commonwealth and becomes a republic.

1962 Nelson Mandela arrested.

1976 Violent riots in Soweto. Later spread to other black areas.

1977 Black community leader Steve Biko dies while in custody.

1986 President P.W. Botha declares state of emergency in response to growing township violence.

1989 P. W. Botha resigns. Replaced by F. W. de Klerk.

1990 F. W. de Klerk announces law to legalize ANC and other banned groups.

1990 Nelson Mandela released from prison.

1992 Scores killed in Boipatong, south of Johannesburg. Mainly Zulu Inkatha Freedom Party supporters blamed.

1992 Security forces kill 28 ANC supporters in Ciskei.

1993 Mandela and de Klerk awarded Nobel Peace Prize.

1994 First multiracial elections.

1996 National Party withdraws from government of national unity.

2004 Third free elections return ANC to power.

BASIC FACTS

OFFICIAL NAME: Republic of South Africa

OFFICAL LANGUAGES: Afrikaans, English, isiNdebele, isiXhosa, isiZulu, Sesotho, Sesotho sa Leboa, Setswana, SiSwati, Tshivenda, Xitsonga

MAJOR RELIGIONS: Christianity, Islam, traditional beliefs

POPULATION: 44.8 million

CAPITAL: Pretoria, Cape Town, Bloemfontein

CURRENCY: Rand (1 Rand = $0.15)

MAJOR INDUSTRIES: Gold and diamond mining, mineral extraction, tourism, manufacturing, food and wine

NATIONAL INCOME: per person $2750

LIFE EXPECTANCY: 47 years (male), 51 years (female)

ADMINISTRATION: Nine provinces: Eastern Cape, Free State, Gauteng, KwaZulu-Natal, Limpopo, Mpumalanga, Northern Cape, North-West, Western Cape

NEIGHBORING COUNTRIES: Botswana, Lesotho, Mozambique, Namibia, Swaziland, Zimbabwe

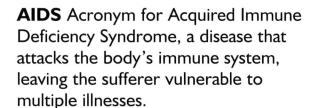

AIDS Acronym for Acquired Immune Deficiency Syndrome, a disease that attacks the body's immune system, leaving the sufferer vulnerable to multiple illnesses.

ANC The African National Congress. Under apartheid, it fought a guerrilla resistance campaign. Today, it has renounced violence to become the ruling political party.

Apartheid The body of laws in South Africa that kept people of different colors separated from each other and discriminated against those who were not white.

Black-majority rule Government by members of the black community, which is the biggest in South Africa.

Boers Dutch-speaking farmers who settled in South Africa.

Cape A very large piece of land jutting out into the sea. In South Africa, the term usually applies to the Cape of Good Hope, where Cape Town is situated.

Constitution The supreme law by which a country is governed.

Gated community A collection of homes with its own secure outside space that nonresidents cannot enter.

HIV Human immunodeficiency virus, the virus that causes AIDS.

Homelands The areas to which black people were restricted under apartheid.

Indentured laborer A person contracted to work, with or without wages, for a certain period of time.

Proportional representation A means of organizing elections in which each candidate gains in direct proportion to the number of votes cast for him. Supporters of proportional representation claim that it is the fairest way to choose leaders.

Shantytown An informal settlement, usually made up of temporary huts.

Townships The impoverished communities in which black and Colored people were resettled under apartheid in order to free up other districts for whites.

Voortrekker Literally, "one who moves the front;" Boer pioneers.

USEFUL WEB SITES

www.southafrica.net

The official South African tourism site.

www.southafrica.co.za

News and articles about South Africa.

www.mg.co.za

Web site of the South African newspaper the *Mail & Guardian*, with national and international news.

www.statssa.gov.za

Statistics and figures about South Africa provided by the government.

www.safrica.info

All-in-one official Web site with news, government information, and articles.

www.sabc.co.za

Web site of South Africa's national broadcast station, the SABC.

www.weathersa.co.za

Online South African weather service.

www.parliament.gov.za

News and information about South Africa's parliament.

Note to parents and teachers:
Every effort has been made to ensure that the Web sites in this book are suitable for children, that they are of the highest educational value, and that they contain no inappropriate or offensive material. However, because of the nature of the Internet, it is impossible to guarantee that the contents of these sites will not be altered. We strongly advise that Internet access be supervised by a responsible adult.